Can you imagine showing up to a wedding—let's say your own—that was not planned in advance by *someone*? Would there be a wedding at all? When recent high school graduates go off to college, no one expects them to arrive on campus the first day of class without having applied, registered, paid tuition, and arranged housing ahead of time.

The expression "If you fail to plan, you are planning to fail," has been attributed to Benjamin Franklin. Smart man. So, if we want to succeed at anything, we'd better design a strategy to do so. Neglecting to do that will certainly lead to failure.

Finances are no different.

Financial planning is simply telling your money where it's going to go before you let it leave. Not one penny departs without your permission and direction. If you want to leave some room for spontaneity, that's fine, just make sure it's in your plan ahead of time.

Planning for a wedding or college takes time, effort, some will power, and perhaps just grit. You will find those resources are necessary in your fiscal endeavors, too.

So, let's get a look at your financial plan. It's never too late to start, even for you.

© Skwiggl Notebooks

skwigglnotebooks@gmail.com

With regard to personal finances, people tend to bury their heads in the sand for one of three reasons: they don't know where they stand, they don't know what to do, or they don't want to change. The fact that you are already on page 3 of this book indicates that you are not in the last category—you WANT to make a change. This book will tell you what to do; so, that just leaves figuring out where you are. And, knowing where you stand is *more than half* the battle. And there is something powerful that comes with **WRITING DOWN** the information as opposed to using an app on your phone. If you're new to this whole budgeting "thing," start here—with a pencil and this notebook.

On the next page, list all your sources of income. Most people only have one or two, and they're called jobs. But there are other types of income that some people tend to forget about, so we're going to help you out with a list of potential income sources:

Wages/Salary from All Jobs

Tips

Child Support and Alimony

Gifts

Investment Income or Royalties

Rental Income

Side/Home-based Business

Disability, Annuity or Settlement Payments

Make notes on the next page (entitled "Notes") of *potential* income sources that you might be interested in investigating further. We'll talk about that later. On page 5, list your income source description on the left and the amount you receive in the corresponding row to the right. If you need more lines, use the following notes page. Be sure to total up each page as you go.

Different forms of income will come in at different times. All our pages are based on monthly figures. Here are some formulas to help you figure out your monthly income amounts:

Monthly: We think this is self explanatory. After all, most bills are due monthly, but not all. We will talk about that, too.

Every other week (aka biweekly): Bi-weekly amount x 26, then divide that amount by 12.

Weekly: Weekly amount x 52, then divide that amount by 12.

Twice monthly: One amount x 2.

Some incomes are paid annually (once a year, but it is very rare): Yearly amount divided by 12.

Tipped employees: **ALWAYS** right down how much you earn in tips **EVERY DAY**. Take the total you collected in a month and divide by the number of days you worked that month. This gives you a monthly average. If you want a more accurate average, do it for more than one month, or even an entire year.

You are going to be working ahead. If this month is January, then the money you are putting aside is going toward February so you're not always trying to play catch up, i.e. paying your January mortgage (due January 1) with money coming in the middle of that same month.

Notes

Income

Description	Amount
Total this page	

Notes

Now, we need to talk about the *ugliest* four-letter word in the English language:

DEBT

Yes, it's awful. But once you can name the enemy, you can beat it. The Merriam-Webster Dictionary has four definitions of the word debt, and none of them are good. The first one is actually synonymous with *sin*. (Perhaps if we all looked at it that way, we would all be a little less inclined to partake!). The second one is *something owed*, and it's never fun to *owe* anybody *anything*. Owing money to anyone robs you of your path to prosperity. So, let's tackle this monster.

Debt is **NOT** an every-day living expense. It is something that once paid for, you don't have to continue to pay for it any more. Things like groceries and electricity are not considered debts. The good thing about debt is it will go away and stay away if you stick to a plan.

You've heard this already, but it needs to be said again. Knowing where you stand is half the battle. On the next 3 pages, list every entity to which you owe any amount of money. Every one of those entities to which you owe money is called a creditor. The description/creditor name goes on the left, the total amount owed to that creditor goes in the corresponding box in the center row, and the monthly payment to the far right. Make sure you get them *all*; here are some suggestions to jog your memory:

Mortgage

Second Mortgage/Home Equity Line of Credit

Student Loans

Credit Cards—VISA, MasterCard, Discover, etc.

Car, Boat, RV and Other Toys Loans, etc.

Store Credit Cards—Kohls, JC Penney, Macy's, etc.

Medical-Hospitals, Doctors, Dentists, etc.

Payday or Title Loans

Personal or Debt-Consolidation Loans

Taxes/IRS

Rent-to-Own Anything

401(k) Loans

You may have noticed that there is no column for the interest rate on the debt you list. If you really want to, you may write it out to the far right of the "Total Owed" column. When you follow the ideas in this book, you will find that interest rates do not make a huge difference for those people who are **REALLY READY** to get out of debt. It is more about behavior than interest rates.

Notes

Debt

Description	Total Owed	Payment
Total this page		

Debt

Description	Total Owed	Payment
Total this page		

Debt

Description	Total Owed	Payment
Total this page		
Total all pages		

Notes

If you have already looked ahead to the next few pages, you might notice that there are three of them that look a little familiar. This was not an accident. These specific pages have a purpose!

Double check all the debts you have listed and make sure that you have all of them.

Now, take the same debts, total owed, and payments from pages 9, 10, and 11, and put them in order from the smallest amount owed (the total balance of what you owe that creditor, **NOT** the smallest payment) and list it on the first line of page 15. When it is relisted, line through it on the original list to indicate it has been moved. Next, do the same thing with the second smallest debt with its balance and payment, crossing it off the original list when it has been relisted. Keep going until you have moved each one and crossed them all off. It will not be necessary to total up amounts again, unless you want to.

Notes

Debt

Description	Total Owed	Payment

Debt

Description	Total Owed	Payment

Debt

Description	Total Owed	Payment

Notes

The next few pages are specifically for living expenses, those items that you will continue to pay for even if you don't owe anybody a thing. If you work for someone besides yourself and receive a paycheck, many of the items listed are automatically taken from your paycheck. There are probably more living expenses than most people realize, so here are some hints:

Charities

Savings—Emergency, Retirement, College Funds

Taxes—Income, Real Estate, Auto

Alimony/Child Support

Child Care

Home Repairs and Association Dues

Medical—Deductibles, Co-Pays, Medications

Utilities—Gas, Electricity, Water, Trash, Phone, etc.

Insurance—Auto, Home, Renters, Life, Health, ID Theft, Disability

Cell Phone, Internet, and Cable

Grocery and Non-grocery Items

Eating Out

Clothing

Gifts/Christmas

Mad Money and Vacations

Pet Supplies

Music Lessons and Sports Activities

Transportation—Gas, Oil, Car Repair, Tires, Car Replacement

It's okay to create a miscellaneous subcategory within any category, as long as every expense (budget item) has been accounted for. After all, it's your money, and you're going to tell it what to do. List all your monthly expenses and the amounts on the next few pages. If you need more room, use the notes page. Keep in mind there are some things that are not paid monthly. Auto insurance can be paid semi-annually (every 6 months). Some property taxes (not included with a mortgage payment) are due yearly, semi-annually, or quarterly. Include in your budget what those items would be if you paid them on a monthly basis. If it's due once a year, divide it by 12. If it's due semi-annually, divide the amount by 6. Make sure you total up each page, then all pages.

Notes

Expenses

Description	Amount
Total this page	

Expenses

Description	Amount
Total this page	

Expenses

Description	Amount
Total this page	
Total all pages	

Notes

There are many people who, once they write down everything and actually stick to their plan, feel like they've gotten a raise. Being in control will do that for you. Add your total monthly debts to your total monthly expenses. They should be less than your monthly income. If they are not, then you have been living way beyond your means and you are probably using credit cards to just "get by" every month. If this is the case, you need to make some fast, hard adjustments to reduce your living expenses and/or get more money coming in. Here are some questions to ask yourself and your significant other:

Is my television service really that important?

Can I eliminate my home phone? Can we find a cheaper cell plan?

What subscriptions are we paying for that we can eliminate?

How much are we eating out? "Having drinks"? Can we brown-bag lunches?

Can we combine trips in the car? Can we sell a car with debt and buy something cheap just to get us around for now?

Can we give up soda/coffee runs, pedicures, expensive haircuts?

How much time do we spend watching TV? Can we (or one of us) find a part-time job?

Can we work opposite shifts to cut down on daycare costs?

Finding ways to reduce expenses is going to be tough—there's no way around it. In addition to reducing costs, there are ways to bring in extra money:

Have a garage sale or find things around the house to sell on eBay, Amazon, Craig's List or Facebook Marketplaces

Get a part-time job—paper routes still exist, or deliver pizzas

Find what you are good at and tutor/teach someone else—do you play an instrument? Are you good in math?

Do yardwork or shovel snow, and dog-sitting is really a thing

Now is a GREAT time to quit smoking

Do you craft? Check out selling things on Etsy

TEMPORARILY stop contributing to your retirement—just till you're out of debt

Change your W4—get less of a tax return and more in your paycheck

Notes

Don't wait until you are upside down to begin any of these strategies. The more you can cut expenses and increase your income, the faster you will be able to get rid of your debt. Now that you know where you stand with income, expenses/budget items, and debt, you can put your plan into action. Every month, you are going to continue to make all of your budget item and debt payments while continuing to live on the cheap. Literally.

But, we are going to tell you to do something first, before you jump right in. Save $1,000 and put it in a savings account. Do not spend it for anything else other than a bona fide **EMERGENCY**. Ever heard of Murphy's Law? It basically says that if anything can go wrong, it will. Well, having this little emergency stash will help keep little things from detracting you from your goal. When you've got that set aside, move forward with the rest of your plan.

Any extra money that you have from your budget or come across from any legal, moral, and ethical source (we are not encouraging bad behavior, here) should be paid on the smallest debt (remember it's the smallest total **BALANCE** owed, not smallest payment). When that smallest debt is **GONE FOR GOOD**, take that monthly amount that you were paying on that smallest debt **PLUS** any other money you can squeeze out and put it on the next largest debt. This principle is called "snowballing." Think about a small snowball rolling down a hill and picking up more snow at it gathers speed. This is what you're doing with your money **AGAINST** your debt.

Most of the remaining pages in this book are for you to be able to track where your money is scheduled to go before you let it leave. Write the name of one budget item or the debt at the top (i.e. Groceries) and the monthly budgeted amount for that category (i.e. $500), each one getting its own page, front and back. Do this for each debt and for each expense.

As you pay off the debts, you can get the satisfaction of **RIPPING OUT THE PAGE** with that debt on it.

As you completely use a page (front and back) for a budget item, just draw a big "X" on the completed page and carry the balance from the bottom of that page to the top of the next one behind it. Use the description "Balance forward" and put the date.

As you add money at the beginning of the month to your budget item or debt, place the date and the description in their proper places, and the amount to be added in the "Debit +" column, then add that to the balance. When money is spent from that budget item or debt, record the amount spent in the "Credit -" column and subtract it from the balance. When there is a zero balance in this page, you have no money to spend for that budget item/debt until you are able to add more from a paycheck or other income source.

On payday when you are adding monthly amounts to the individual budget items/debts, as you go, subtract each monthly amount from the amount of your paycheck. Continue adding monthly amounts to individual budget items and debts until the amount of your left in your paycheck equals zero. If you have filled in every budget item/debt monthly and have money left over, add that to the smallest debt you currently have—it will get paid off that much faster.

Notes

Name: **Monthly Amount:**

Date	Description	Debit +	Credit -	Balance

Name: **Monthly Amount:**

Name:			Monthly Amount:		
Date	Description		Debit +	Credit -	Balance
Name:			Monthly Amount:		

Name:			Monthly Amount:	
Date	Description	Debit +	Credit -	Balance

Name:			Monthly Amount:		
Date	Description	Debit +	Credit -	Balance	

Name:			Monthly Amount:		
Date	Description		Debit +	Credit -	Balance
Name:			Monthly Amount:		

Name:			Monthly Amount:	
Date	**Description**	**Debit +**	**Credit -**	**Balance**

Name:			Monthly Amount:		
Date	Description		Debit +	Credit -	Balance

Name:			Monthly Amount:		
Date	Description	Debit +	Credit -	Balance	

Name:			Monthly Amount:	

Date	Description	Debit +	Credit -	Balance
			Monthly Amount:	

Name:			Monthly Amount:	
Date	**Description**	**Debit +**	**Credit -**	**Balance**
Name:			Monthly Amount:	

Name:			Monthly Amount:		
Date	Description		Debit +	Credit -	Balance
Name:					

Name:			Monthly Amount:		
Date	Description		Debit +	Credit -	Balance

Name:			Monthly Amount:		
Date	Description	Debit +	Credit -	Balance	
Name:					

Name:			Monthly Amount:		
Date	Description		Debit +	Credit -	Balance

Name:			Monthly Amount:		
Date	Description	Debit +	Credit -	Balance	
		Monthly Amount:			

Name:			Monthly Amount:		
Date	Description	Debit +	Credit -	Balance	

Name:			Monthly Amount:		
Date	Description		Debit +	Credit -	Balance
Name:					

Name:			Monthly Amount:		
Date	Description		Debit +	Credit -	Balance

Name:			Monthly Amount:		
Date	Description		Debit +	Credit -	Balance
	Monthly Amount:				

Name:			Monthly Amount:		
Date	Description		Debit +	Credit -	Balance

Name:			Monthly Amount:		
Date	Description		Debit +	Credit -	Balance
Name:			Monthly Amount:		

Name:			Monthly Amount:		
Date	Description		Debit +	Credit -	Balance

Name:			Monthly Amount:		
Date	Description	Debit +	Credit -	Balance

Name:			Monthly Amount:		
Date	Description		Debit +	Credit -	Balance

Name:			Monthly Amount:		
Date	Description		Debit +	Credit -	Balance
Name:					

Name:			Monthly Amount:		
Date	Description		Debit +	Credit -	Balance

Name:			Monthly Amount:		
Date	Description		Debit +	Credit -	Balance
			Monthly Amount:		

Name:			Monthly Amount:		
Date	Description	Debit +	Credit -	Balance	

Name:			Monthly Amount:		
Date	Description		Debit +	Credit -	Balance

Name:			Monthly Amount:		
Date	Description		Debit +	Credit -	Balance

Name:			Monthly Amount:		
Date	Description		Debit +	Credit -	Balance
		Monthly Amount:			

Name:			Monthly Amount:		
Date	Description		Debit +	Credit -	Balance

Name:			Monthly Amount:		
Date	Description		Debit +	Credit -	Balance
			Monthly Amount:		

Name:			Monthly Amount:		
Date	Description		Debit +	Credit -	Balance

Name:			Monthly Amount:		
Date	Description	Debit +	Credit -	Balance	
Name:			Monthly Amount:		

Name:			Monthly Amount:		
Date	Description		Debit +	Credit -	Balance

Name:			Monthly Amount:		
Date	Description		Debit +	Credit -	Balance
Name:			Monthly Amount:		

Name:			Monthly Amount:		
Date	Description		Debit +	Credit -	Balance

Name:			Monthly Amount:		
Date	Description	Debit +	Credit -	Balance	
Name:					

Name:			Monthly Amount:		
Date	Description		Debit +	Credit -	Balance

Name:			Monthly Amount:		
Date	Description		Debit +	Credit -	Balance
Name:					

Name:				Monthly Amount:	
Date	Description		Debit +	Credit -	Balance

Name:			Monthly Amount:		
Date	Description	Debit +	Credit -	Balance

Name:			Monthly Amount:		
Date	Description	Debit +	Credit -	Balance	

Name:			Monthly Amount:		
Date	Description	Debit +	Credit -	Balance
Name:					

Name:			Monthly Amount:	
Date	Description	Debit +	Credit -	Balance

Name:			Monthly Amount:	
Date	Description	Debit +	Credit -	Balance

Name:			Monthly Amount:	
Date	**Description**	**Debit +**	**Credit -**	**Balance**

Name:			Monthly Amount:		
Date	Description	Debit +	Credit -	Balance	
Name:			Monthly Amount:		

Name:			Monthly Amount:		
Date	Description	Debit +	Credit -	Balance	

Name: **Monthly Amount:**

Date	Description	Debit +	Credit -	Balance
	Monthly Amount:			

Name: **Monthly Amount:**

Date	Description	Debit +	Credit -	Balance

Name:			Monthly Amount:		
Date	Description		Debit +	Credit -	Balance
Name:					

Name:			Monthly Amount:		
Date	Description	Debit +	Credit -	Balance	
Name:			Monthly Amount:		

Name:			Monthly Amount:		
Date	Description	Debit +	Credit -	Balance	
Name:					

Name:			Monthly Amount:		
Date	**Description**		**Debit +**	**Credit −**	**Balance**

Name:			Monthly Amount:		
Date	Description		Debit +	Credit -	Balance
Name:			Monthly Amount:		

Name:			Monthly Amount:		
Date	Description		Debit +	Credit -	Balance

Name:			Monthly Amount:		
Date	Description	Debit +	Credit -	Balance	

Name:			Monthly Amount:		
Date	Description		Debit +	Credit -	Balance

Name:			Monthly Amount:		
Date	Description	Debit +	Credit -	Balance	
Name:					

Name:			Monthly Amount:		
Date	**Description**		**Debit +**	**Credit -**	**Balance**

Name:			Monthly Amount:		
Date	Description	Debit +	Credit -	Balance	

Name: **Monthly Amount:**

Date	Description	Debit +	Credit -	Balance

Name:			Monthly Amount:		
Date	Description		Debit +	Credit -	Balance
Name:					

Name:			Monthly Amount:		
Date	Description		Debit +	Credit -	Balance

Name:			Monthly Amount:		
Date	Description	Debit +	Credit -	Balance	
		Monthly Amount:			

Name: **Monthly Amount:**

Date	Description	Debit +	Credit -	Balance

Name:			Monthly Amount:	
Date	**Description**	**Debit +**	**Credit -**	**Balance**

Name:			Monthly Amount:		
Date	Description		Debit +	Credit -	Balance

Name:			Monthly Amount:		
Date	Description	Debit +	Credit -	Balance	
		Monthly Amount:			

Name:			Monthly Amount:		
Date	Description	Debit +	Credit -	Balance	

Name:			Monthly Amount:	
Date	Description	Debit +	Credit -	Balance

Name:			Monthly Amount:		
Date	Description		Debit +	Credit -	Balance

Name:			Monthly Amount:		
Date	Description		Debit +	Credit -	Balance

Name:			Monthly Amount:	
Date	**Description**	**Debit +**	**Credit -**	**Balance**

Name:			Monthly Amount:		
Date	Description		Debit +	Credit -	Balance

Name:			Monthly Amount:		
Date	Description		Debit +	Credit -	Balance

Name:			Monthly Amount:	
Date	Description	Debit +	Credit -	Balance

Name:			Monthly Amount:		
Date	Description		Debit +	Credit -	Balance

Name:			Monthly Amount:		
Date	Description	Debit +	Credit -	Balance	

Name:			Monthly Amount:		
Date	Description		Debit +	Credit -	Balance

Name:			Monthly Amount:		
Date	Description	Debit +	Credit -	Balance	
Name:			Monthly Amount:		

Name:			Monthly Amount:		
Date	Description		Debit +	Credit -	Balance

Name:			Monthly Amount:	

Date	Description	Debit +	Credit -	Balance

Name:			Monthly Amount:		
Date	Description		Debit +	Credit -	Balance

Name:			Monthly Amount:		
Date	Description	Debit +	Credit -	Balance	

Name: **Monthly Amount:**

Date	Description	Debit +	Credit -	Balance

Name:			Monthly Amount:		
Date	Description	Debit +	Credit -	Balance	

Name:			Monthly Amount:		
Date	Description		Debit +	Credit -	Balance
Name:			Monthly Amount:		

Name:			Monthly Amount:		
Date	Description		Debit +	Credit -	Balance
			Monthly Amount:		

Name:			Monthly Amount:		
Date	Description	Debit +	Credit -	Balance

Name:			Monthly Amount:		
Date	Description		Debit +	Credit -	Balance
Name:					

Name:			Monthly Amount:		
Date	Description		Debit +	Credit -	Balance

Name:			Monthly Amount:		
Date	Description		Debit +	Credit -	Balance

Name:			Monthly Amount:		
Date	Description		Debit +	Credit -	Balance

Name:			Monthly Amount:		
Date	Description		Debit +	Credit -	Balance
Name:					

Name:			Monthly Amount:		
Date	Description		Debit +	Credit -	Balance

Name:			Monthly Amount:		
Date	Description	Debit +	Credit -	Balance	

Name:			Monthly Amount:		
Date	Description		Debit +	Credit -	Balance

Name:			Monthly Amount:		
Date	Description		Debit +	Credit -	Balance

Name:			Monthly Amount:		
Date	Description		Debit +	Credit -	Balance

Name:			Monthly Amount:		
Date	Description	Debit +	Credit -	Balance	

Name:			Monthly Amount:		
Date	Description		Debit +	Credit -	Balance

Name:			Monthly Amount:		
Date	Description	Debit +	Credit -	Balance	

Name:			Monthly Amount:		
Date	Description		Debit +	Credit -	Balance

Name:			Monthly Amount:		
Date	Description		Debit +	Credit -	Balance

Name:			Monthly Amount:		
Date	Description	Debit +	Credit -	Balance
Name:					

Name:			Monthly Amount:		
Date	Description		Debit +	Credit -	Balance

Notes

When you have used up all the pages in the book, just grab another book. This is the method I have used to become debt free, and it's still the method I use to stay within my budget so that I remain debt free.

I will share a secret with you that I have seen time and time again. When we have the desire to manage our money, make a plan, and stick to it, somehow, we receive divine intervention, providence, karma, or whatever you want to call it. Things happen to help us achieve our goals. While money is not the most important thing in life, finances play a huge part of our overall well-being. Becoming debt-free is hard work and doesn't happen over night, but it is the first step toward building a comfortable financial future. And, who doesn't want that?

You can make your money behave. Go ahead. I dare you.

© Skwiggl Notebooks

skwigglnotebooks@gmail.com

www.ingramcontent.com/pod-product-compliance
Lightning Source LLC
Chambersburg PA
CBHW080943240526
45469CB00018B/2617